ORGAN MUSIC FOR MANUALS BOOK 4

Edited by C. H. TREVOR

NOTE

Stops with the same names do not always produce the same effect on different organs. Other registrations should be used if those suggested are not effective or suitable on any particular instrument. The directions in brackets may be used or not at the player's discretion.

All the pieces can be played effectively on a one-manual organ with appropriate stops.

The pedals can be used at the player's discretion.

C.H.T.

CONTENTS

TWO PIECES

John Alcock (1715—1806)

No. 1. Diapason Movement
(from a voluntary)

Gt. light Diapasons 8. 4.

No. 2. Trumpet Piece

This piece was written when the composer was organist of St. Andrew's Church, Plymouth.

R.H. Trumpet 8.
L.H. 8. 4. (2.)

© Oxford University Press 1973

Printed in Great Britain

OXFORD UNIVERSITY PRESS, MUSIC DEPARTMENT, GREAT CLARENDON STREET, OXFORD OX2 6DP
Photocopying this copyright material is ILLEGAL.

(2nd time rall.)

Interlude

Charles Alexis Chauvet (1837—1871)

Sw. Voix Céleste 8.

Adagio e sostenuto

espressivo

rit.

4

TWO PIECES

Johann Pachelbel (1653—1706)

No. 1. Fugue No. 5.
(Magnificat primi toni)

light Diapasons (or Flutes) 8. 4. (2.)

(rall.)

No. 2. Chorale prelude, "Christe, der du bist Tag und Licht"

Gt. light Diapason 8.

Diapason Movement
(from a voluntary)

George Green
(18th century)

Gt. light Diapason 8.

Ricercare per Organo

Floriano Arresti (1650—1719)

I Gt. light Diapasons 8. 4. (2.)
II Ch. (or Sw.) 8. 4. 2. (box open.)
(Sw. to Gt.)

If preferred, this piece can be played throughout on Great uncoupled or coupled to Swell.

(allargando)

TWO PIECES

Jacques Boyvin (1653—1706)

No. 1. Dialogue du deuxième ton

No. 2. Trio du premier ton

R.H. Gt. (or Ch.) Flute(s) 8. (4.)
L.H. Sw. Oboe (or Diapason) 8. (Principal 4.)

Alternative registration:
Ch. (or Gt.) Flutes 8. 4. both hands.

Fughetta in A

Johann Christian Kittel (1732—1809)
pupil of J. S. Bach

Gt. Diapasons 8. 4.

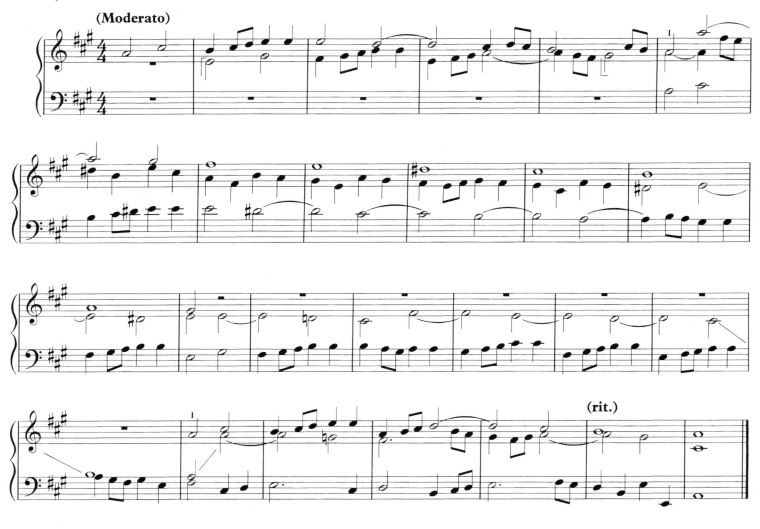

TWO PIECES

Georg Philipp Telemann (1681—1767)

No. 1. Chorale prelude (bicinium), "Alle Menschen müssen sterben"

R.H. Ch. Cornet (8. 4. 2⅔. 2. 1⅗.)
L.H. Sw. 8. (4.) 2.

Alternative registration:
Gt. (or Ch.) Flutes 8. 4. both hands.

Organ Music for Manuals (Book IV)

Organ Music for Manuals (Book IV)

No. 2. Fughetta in D

Gt. Diapasons 8. 4.

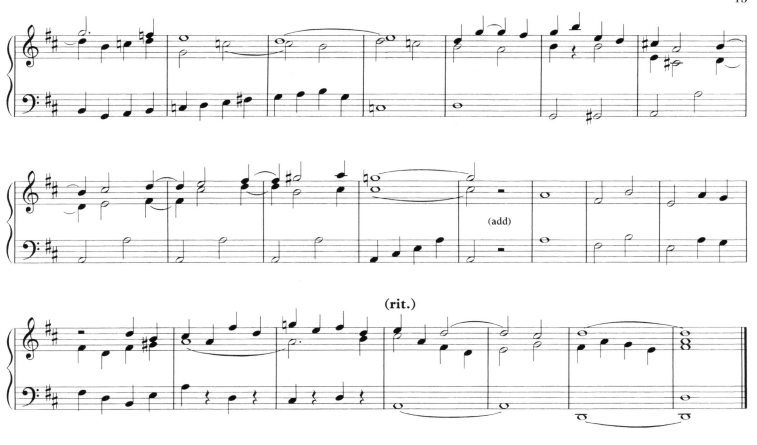

Praeludium

Johann Christian Rinck (1770–1846)

Chorale prelude, "Allein Gott in der Höh' sei Ehr'"

Georg Michael Telemann (1748—1841)
grandson of G. P. Telemann

Gt. light 8. 4. (2.)

(Allegretto)

Organ Music for Manuals (Book IV)

Hymnus, "Jam lucis orto sydere"

Thomas Tallis (1505—1585)

Gt. light Diapasons 8. 4. (2.)

Chorale prelude, "Herr Jesu Christ, wahr' Mensch und Gott"

Friedrich Wilhelm Zachau (1663—1712)
teacher of Handel

Gt. light Diapasons (or Flutes) 8. 4.

(Moderato)

Organ Music for Manuals (Book IV)

Communion

César Franck (1822—1890)

Sw. soft 8.

Verset

Nicolas Gigault (1625—1707)

Sw. Diapason 8.

Fugue on B.A.C.H.

Georg Andreas Sorge (1703—1778)

Gt. Diapasons 8. 4.

(Moderato)

(rall.)

Organ Music for Manuals (Book IV)

Ricercare cromatico per Organo

Tarquinio Merula (1590—1665)

(poco a poco rall.)

Verset

Louis Marchand (1669 – 1732)

Gt. Diapason 8.

(Adagio)

(rit.)

TWO PIECES

Léon Boëllmann (1862–1897)

No. 1. Pastorale

Sw. soft 8.

No. 2. Postlude

Ped. *(ad lib.)*

3 VERSILLOS

Anonymous
(17th century)

No. 1. Primer Tono

No. 2. Segundo Tono

No. 3. Tercer Tono

Registrations for each of the above: Diapason 8. or Flutes 8. 4.

Cornet Voluntary

Henry Heron
(18th century)

Slow

Gt. light Diapason 8.

(rall.)

Allegro

★ I Cornet (8. 4. 2⅔. 2. 1⅗.)

II 8. 4. (2.)

II

I

sempre II

II

I

★Alternative registration for a one-manual organ: light 8. 4. (2.)

Organ Music for Manuals (Book IV)

Adagio
(from a voluntary)

John Stanley (1713—1786)

Sw. Flute (or Diapason) 8.